THE GREATEST PLAYERS

TENNIS

Steve Goldsworthy

MEDIA ENHANCED BOOKS
AV2 BY WEIGL™
ADDED VALUE • AUDIO VISUAL

AV² provides enriched content that supplements and complements this book. Weigl's AV² books strive to create inspired learning and engage young minds in a total learning experience.

Your AV² Media Enhanced books come alive with...

Audio
Listen to sections of the book read aloud.

Key Words
Study vocabulary, and complete a matching word activity.

Go to **www.av2books.com**, and enter this book's unique code.

Video
Watch informative video clips.

Quizzes
Test your knowledge.

BOOK CODE

C 2 1 6 3 8 8

Embedded Weblinks
Gain additional information for research.

Slide Show
View images and captions, and prepare a presentation.

AV² by Weigl brings you media enhanced books that support active learning.

Try This!
Complete activities and hands-on experiments.

... and much, much more!

Published by AV² by Weigl
350 5th Avenue, 59th Floor
New York, NY 10118
Website: www.av2books.com   www.weigl.com

Library of Congress Cataloging-in-Publication Data
Goldsworthy, Steve.
 Tennis / Steve Goldsworthy.
    p. cm. -- (The greatest players)
 Includes index.
 ISBN 978-1-62127-504-6 (hardcover : alk. paper) -- ISBN 978-1-62127-507-7 (softcover : alk. paper)
 1. Tennis players--Biography--Juvenile literature. I. Title.
 GV994.A1G65 2012
 796.3420922--dc23

 [B]

                          2012045103

Printed in the United States of America in North Mankato, Minnesota
1 2 3 4 5 6 7 8 9 0 17 16 15 14 13

032013
WEP300113

Project Coordinator Aaron Carr
Editor Steve Macleod
Art Director Terry Paulhus

Photo Credits
Every reasonable effort has been made to trace ownership and to obtain permission to reprint copyright material. The publishers would be pleased to have any errors or omissions brought to their attention so that they may be corrected in subsequent printings.

Weigl acknowledges Getty Images as its primary image supplier for this title.

Contents

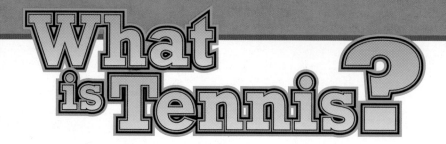
What is Tennis?

Introduction

The world of **professional** sports has a long history of great moments. The most memorable moments often come when the sport's greatest players overcome challenging obstacles. For the fans, these moments come to define their favorite sport. For the players, they stand as measuring posts of success.

The first **Wimbledon Championships** were held in 1877. Since then, there have been many great players and great moments at tennis tournaments around the world. These moments include Billie Jean King defeating a male tennis player in an exhibition match and Roger Federer's 17 **Grand Slam** titles. Tennis has no shortage of these moments, when the sport's brightest stars accomplished feats that ensured they would be remembered as the greatest players.

Warm Up

A **singles** match involves two players. The game starts with a **serve**. The player serving has two chances to hit the ball over the net into the service box. The ball can bounce once before it must be hit back over the net. Players hit the ball back and forth until someone misses the ball or hits it out of bounds. When this happens, the other player gets a point.

Four points win a game. The first point is called 15, the second 30, and the third 40. A game tied at 40-40 is called deuce. Players must win a game by two points. Players must win six games to win a set. In men's tournaments, it takes three sets to win a match. In women's and **doubles** tournaments, it takes two sets to win a match.

Serena Williams was the number one ranked female tennis player in the world at the end of 2002 and 2009.

The Tennis Court

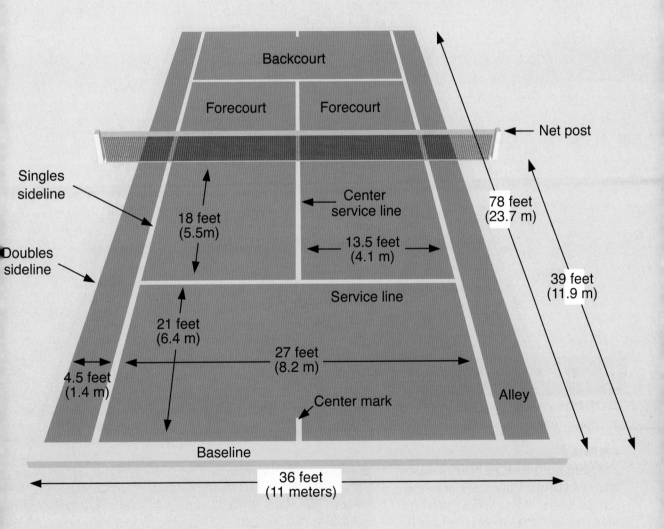

Backcourt

Forecourt   Forecourt

Net post

Singles sideline

18 feet (5.5m)

Center service line

Doubles sideline

13.5 feet (4.1 m)

78 feet (23.7 m)

Service line

21 feet (6.4 m)

39 feet (11.9 m)

4.5 feet (1.4 m)

27 feet (8.2 m)

Center mark

Alley

Baseline

36 feet (11 meters)

"I wanted to win, even in practice."

Björn Borg

Player Profile

BORN Björn Rune Borg was born on June 6, 1956, in Södertälje, Sweden.

FAMILY Borg was the only child of Rune and Margaretha Borg. He married and divorced Mariana Simionescu, as well as Loredana Berte. Borg got married for the third time in 2002 to Patricia Ostfeldt. He has two sons, Robin and Leo.

EDUCATION Borg left school at age 15 to play tennis full-time.

AWARDS Borg won 11 Grand Slam singles titles. He was inducted into the International Tennis Hall of Fame in 1987.

Björn Borg was nicknamed the "Ice Man" because he stayed calm even when there was a lot of pressure during a tennis match.

Björn Borg
Sweden

Early Years

Björn Borg's father received a tennis racket for winning a **table tennis** tournament. Borg soon started playing tennis with the racket. He developed a powerful **forehand** and **backhand**. Borg won his first tournament when he was 11 years old. He was winning matches against the best junior players in Sweden by age 13.

Borg played for Sweden at the **Davis Cup** in 1972. He was only 15 years old. He became the youngest singles player ever to compete in the tournament. Borg won his first match in five sets. That year, he also won the boys' junior tournament at Wimbledon. Borg joined the **Association of Tennis Professionals (ATP)** Tour in 1973. He did not win an event that year, but he did make it to the final round of four tournaments.

Developing Skills

Borg won his first ATP tournament in 1974. He won eight tournaments that year. Borg also won his first Grand Slam tournament in 1974. It was at the **French Open**. He lost the first two sets in the final to Manuel Orantes of Spain. He came back to win the match in five sets.

Borg won the French Open six times. He set the record for most men's singles titles at the event. In 1976, Borg won his first Wimbledon singles title at age 20. He won all seven rounds without losing a single set. Borg became the youngest player ever to win the Wimbledon men's singles title. He won the event again every years from 1977 to 1980. It set a record for most consecutive Wimbledon titles. Borg won 64 ATP tournaments during his career. He retired from professional tennis in 1983. He was only 26 years old.

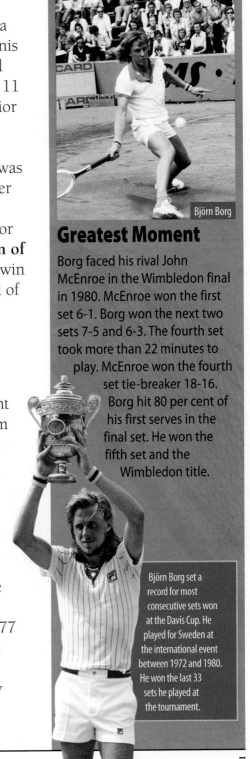

Björn Borg

Greatest Moment

Borg faced his rival John McEnroe in the Wimbledon final in 1980. McEnroe won the first set 6-1. Borg won the next two sets 7-5 and 6-3. The fourth set took more than 22 minutes to play. McEnroe won the fourth set tie-breaker 18-16. Borg hit 80 per cent of his first serves in the final set. He won the fifth set and the Wimbledon title.

Björn Borg set a record for most consecutive sets won at the Davis Cup. He played for Sweden at the international event between 1972 and 1980. He won the last 33 sets he played at the tournament.

> "The mark of a good sportsman is not how good they are at their best, but how good they are at their worst."
>
> Martina Navratilova

Martina Navratilova was on the WTA Doubles Team of the Year 11 times.

Player Profile

BORN Martina Šubertová was born on October 18, 1956, in Prague, Czech Republic.

FAMILY She was born to Miroslav Subert and Jana Šubertová. She has a sister named Jana.

EDUCATION She left the Czech Republic during high school to live in the United States and play tennis full-time.

AWARDS Navratilova won 18 Grand Slam singles titles. She also won 31 Grand Slam doubles titles and 10 Grand Slam mixed doubles titles. Navratilova was named the **Women's Tennis Association (WTA)** Player of the Year in 1978, 1979, 1982, 1983, 1984, 1985, and 1986. She was inducted into the International Tennis Hall of Fame in 2000.

Martina Navratilova
United States

Early Years

Martina's grandmother was an international tennis player. Her parents divorced when she was 3 years old. By age 4, Marina started hitting tennis balls against a wall. Her mother married Miroslav Navrátil in 1962, and Martina changed her last name to Navratilova. Her step father then became Navratilova's first tennis coach.

Navratilova began taking lessons from Czech tennis champion George Parma at age 9. At 15, she won the Czech national tennis championship. Navratilova became a professional tennis player the next year. She played on the United States Lawn Tennis Association tour. After the **U.S. Open** in 1975, she stayed in the United States. She was 18.

Developing Skills

Navratilova won her first Grand Slam title at Wimbledon in 1978, defeating Chris Evert in three sets. She became the number one ranked tennis player in the world. She won Wimbledon again the next year, and her third Grand Slam title at the **Australian Open** in 1981.

Navratilova won many Grand Slam titles between 1982 and 1984, including eight singles titles and 10 doubles titles. During that time, she only lost six singles matches. She played in the Wimbledon singles final 12 times and won the event a record nine times. Navratilova also holds the record for most singles titles, with 167, and career doubles titles, with 177.

Martina Navratilova

Greatest Moment

Navratilova lost to Steffi Graf in the final of the French Open in 1987. Later that year, she defeated Graf in the final at Wimbledon. She defeated Graf again to win the U.S. Open that year. She also won the women's doubles title and the mixed doubles title at the U.S. Open in 1987. She became the third player to win three titles at one Grand Slam event.

Just before turning 50, Martina Navratilova won the mixed doubles championship with Bob Bryan at the U.S. Open in 2006. She became the oldest player ever to win a Grand Slam title.

9

"If you don't practice, you don't deserve to win."

Andre Agassi

The Andre Agassi Charitable Foundation has raised more than $150 million since it was created in 1994.

Player Profile

BORN Andre Kirk Agassi was born on April 29, 1970, in Las Vegas, Nevada.

FAMILY Agassi was born to Mike and Elizabeth Agassi. He has an older brother named Phillip, and two older sisters, Rita and Tami. Agassi was married to actress Brooke Shields from 1997 to 1999. He married Steffi Graf in 2001. They have a son named Jaden Gil and a daughter named Jaz Elle.

EDUCATION Agassi left school at age 14 to play tennis full-time.

AWARDS Agassi won eight Grand Slam singles titles. He won a gold medal at the 1996 Olympic Games in Atlanta. He was named the ATP Comeback Player of the Year in 1998 and the ATP Player of the Year in 1999. Agassi was inducted into the International Tennis Hall of Fame in 2011.

Andre Agassi
United States

Early Years

Andre Agassi's father was a boxer. He competed in the 1948 and 1952 Olympic Games for Iran. He moved to Las Vegas and built a tennis court in his backyard. He taught all his children to play tennis. Agassi was given his first tennis racket when he was 2 years old. He hit about 3,000 tennis balls a day while growing up. Agassi was winning tournaments by age 10. He defeated future professionals Pete Sampras, Jim Courier, and Michael Chang.

Agassi was sent to Florida when he was 14 years old. He trained at the Nick Bolletieri Tennis Academy. He won several junior national titles. In 1986, he became a professional tennis player at age 16.

Developing Skills

Agassi became known for his colorful clothes and long hair. He won his first ATP Tour title in 1987. It was at a tournament in Brazil. He won six tournaments in 1988. He also reached the semi-final of the French Open and the U.S. Open that year. He finished the year as the number three ranked player on the ATP Tour.

Agassi won his first Grand Slam title at Wimbledon in 1992. He defeated former champions Boris Becker and John McEnroe to get to the final. He defeated Goran Ivanisevic in five sets to win the title. Agassi won his second Grand Slam title at the U.S. Open in 1994. He won the Australian Open in 1995. He became the number one ranked player in the world that year. Agassi retired from tennis in 2006. He won 60 ATP Tour events during his career.

Andre Agassi

Greatest Moment

Agassi hit a **slump** in 1997. He was ranked as low as 141 that year. The next year he won five titles. He also reached the final round in five other tournaments. He finished the year ranked number six. It was the biggest jump into the top 10 in the history of the ATP rankings.

Agassi won the French Open for the first time in 1999. He lost the first two sets in the final to Andrei Medvedev. He came back to win the match in five sets. Agassi won the men's singles title at every Grand Slam event. He is one of only seven male tennis players to complete the career Grand Slam.

Andre Agassi won more than $30 million from tournaments on the ATP Tour. It is the fourth most in history, behind Roger Federer, Pete Sampras, and Rafael Nadal.

> "If you're a champion, you have to have it in your heart."

Chris Evert

Player Profile

BORN Christine Marie Evert was born on December 21, 1954, in Fort Lauderdale, Florida.

FAMILY Evert was born to Jimmy Evert and Colette Thompson. She has four siblings. Evert was married to John Lloyd from 1979 to 1987. She was married to Andy Mills from 1988 to 2006. They had three sons together: Alexander, Nicholas, and Colton. Evert was married to golfer Greg Norman from 2008 to 2009.

EDUCATION Evert graduated from St. Thomas Aquinas High School in Fort Lauderdale, Florida.

AWARDS Evert won 18 Grand Slam singles titles. She also won three Grand Slam doubles titles. Evert was named the Associated Press Female Athlete of the Year in 1974, 1975, 1977, and 1980. She was named the WTA Player of the Year in 1981. She served as president of the WTA from 1982 to 1991. Evert was inducted into the International Tennis Hall of Fame in 1995.

Chris Evert was the number one ranked women's tennis player in the world during seven different seasons.

Chris Evert
United States

Early Years

Chris Evert's father worked as a tennis professional. He began coaching Evert when she was 5 years old. Evert's mother was also a former tennis player. She played matches with Evert every Tuesday and Thursday. By age 11, Evert was winning matches against her mother.

Evert won six U.S. junior national titles. She was still an **amateur** player when she entered the U.S. Open in 1971. She won her first four matches and made it to the semi-final round. She lost that match to Billie Jean King. Evert was 16 years old. She became the youngest player ever to reach the semi-final of the U.S. Open. She became a professional tennis player in December 1972.

Developing Skills

Evert won 12 tournaments in her first season as a professional. She also made it to the final of two Grand Slam events in 1973. She lost the French Open to Margaret Court and Wimbledon to Billie Jean King. The next year, Evert won 55 straight matches. During that stretch she won 10 tournaments in a row, including the French Open and Wimbledon. In total during 1974, Evert won 103 matches and only lost seven. She was the third player in history to win more than 100 matches in a season.

Between 1973 and 1979, Evert set a record for most consecutive matches won on a clay court. She won 125 in a row. She won 24 tournaments in that time. Evert was the first player to win 1,000 singles matches. She retired at the U.S. Open in 1989. She won 1,309 matches and 157 singles titles during her career.

Chris Evert

Greatest Moment

Evert went to a tournament without her parents for the first time when she was 15 years old. It was a small event in North Carolina. Evert played a match against Margaret Court, who was the number one ranked women's tennis player in the world. Evert won the match 7-6, 7-6.

Evert faced her rival Martina Navratilova in the final of the French Open in 1986. Evert won the match in three sets. It was Evert's seventh victory at the French Open, which is a record for the most women's singles titles at the tournament.

Chris Evert reached at least the semi-final round in 52 of the 56 Grand Slam events she entered. She set a record for both men and women by winning at least one Grand Slam title in 13 straight years between 1974 and 1986.

> "The time your game is most vulnerable is when you're ahead; never let up."
>
> Rod Laver

The Australian Open is held at Melbourne Park. The center court was renamed Rod Laver Arena in 2001.

Player Profile

BORN Rodney George Laver was born on August 9, 1938, in Rockhampton, Australia.

FAMILY Laver was born to Roy and Melba Laver. He has two older brothers and a younger sister. Laver married Mary Bensen in 1966. They had one son together. Mary had a daughter and two sons from a previous marriage.

EDUCATION Laver left school at age 15 to play tennis full-time.

AWARDS Laver won 11 Grand Slam singles titles. He also won six Grand Slam doubles titles and three Grand Slam mixed doubles titles. Laver was inducted into the International Tennis Hall of Fame in 1981.

Rod Laver
Australia

Early Years

Rod Laver's parents met while playing tennis. The family had a tennis court at every house they lived in when Laver was growing up. His parents taught all four of their children to play tennis. When Laver was 13 years old, he lost the Central Queensland junior title against one of his older brothers. Laver started training with Australia's Davis Cup captain Harry Hopman. At age 15, Laver dropped out of school and left home to train full-time.

Laver traveled to the United States when he was 17 years old to play tennis. He won the U.S. junior championship in 1956. Laver won his first Grand Slam titles as a doubles player. He won the Australian doubles title and the Wimbledon mixed doubles title in 1959. Laver won his first Grand Slam singles title in 1960 at the Australian Open. At the time, professional players were not allowed to compete in the Grand Slam tournaments or in the Davis Cup. Laver continued to compete as an amateur tennis player.

Developing Skills

Laver won 19 singles tournaments in 1962. He finished the season winning 134 matches and losing only 15. That year, he won the singles title at the Australian Open, the French Open, Wimbledon, and the U.S. Open. He became the second male tennis player in history to win all four Grand Slam titles. Laver became a professional tennis player the next year.

Tennis rules were changed in 1968 to allow professional players to compete in Grand Slam tournaments. This was the start of the "Open Era." Laver won 47 titles as a professional. During his amateur and professional career, Laver won 184 singles titles.

Rod Laver

Greatest Moment

Laver won 17 singles titles in 1969. That year, he also won all four Grand Slam tournaments for a second time. He is the only player in history to complete the career Grand Slam as an amateur and as a professional.

In 1973, professional players were allowed to compete in the Davis Cup. Laver was 35 and had not competed in the tournament since 1962. He won his first singles match in five sets. He played with John Newcombe to win the doubles match in the third round. Australia won all five rounds against the United States to win the Davis Cup.

Rod Laver won 20 matches and lost only four at Davis Cup events during his career. He helped Australia win the international tournament five times.

> "Sports teaches you character, it teaches you to play by the rules, it teaches you to know what it feels like to win and lose. It teaches you about life."

Billie Jean King

Player Profile

BORN Billie Jean Moffitt was born on November 22, 1943, in Long Beach, California.

FAMILY She was born to Bill and Betty Moffitt. She has a brother named Randy. She was married to Lawrence King from 1965 to 1987. She changed her last name to King when they married, but she did not change it back when they divorced.

EDUCATION King graduated from Long Beach Polytechnic High School. She attended California State University, Los Angeles.

AWARDS King won 12 Grand Slam singles titles. She also won 16 Grand Slam doubles titles and 11 Grand Slam mixed doubles titles. King was inducted into the International Tennis Hall of Fame in 1987. She was awarded the **Fed Cup Award of Excellence** in 2010.

In 1972, Billie Jean King became the first female athlete named the *Sports Illustrated* Sportsman of the Year. In 2009, she also became the first female athlete ever to be awarded the Presidential Medal of Freedom.

Billie Jean King
United States

Early Years

Billie Jean King played softball and football before she tried tennis. She had her first group tennis lesson at a public court near her house when she was 11 years old. At age 15, King played in her first Grand Slam at the 1959 U.S. Open. She lost in the first round. The next year, King won her first tournament against adult players at the Philadelphia and District Women's Grass Court Championships.

In 1961, King teamed up with Karen Hantze Susman to compete in the Wimbledon doubles competition. Susman was 19 years old and King was 17. They won the tournament. They became the youngest women's doubles champions in the history of Wimbledon. King left university in her junior year to play tennis full-time.

Developing Skills

King won the Wimbledon doubles title again in 1962. She won the U.S. Open doubles title in 1964. She won her first Grand Slam singles title at Wimbledon in 1966. After that victory, King became the number one ranked women's tennis player in the world.

King won 39 Grand Slam titles, including doubles and mixed doubles titles. In 1971, she became the first female athlete to earn $100,000 in prize money during one year. King fought to make payments the same for men's and women's tournament champions. In 1973, the U.S. Open became the first major tournament to offer equal prizes for men and women.

Billie Jean King

Greatest Moment

Bobby Riggs won the Wimbledon men's singles title in 1939. Three decades later he said that women tennis players were not as good as men. He challenged King to a match in 1973. They competed in an event called the "Battle of the Sexes" in Houston, Texas. About 30,000 people were at the match. Another 50 million people watched it on television. King defeated Riggs in three straight sets: 6-4, 6-3, 6-3.

The U.S. Open is played at the USTA National Tennis Center. In 2006, it was renamed the USTA Billie Jean King National Tennis Center in her honor.

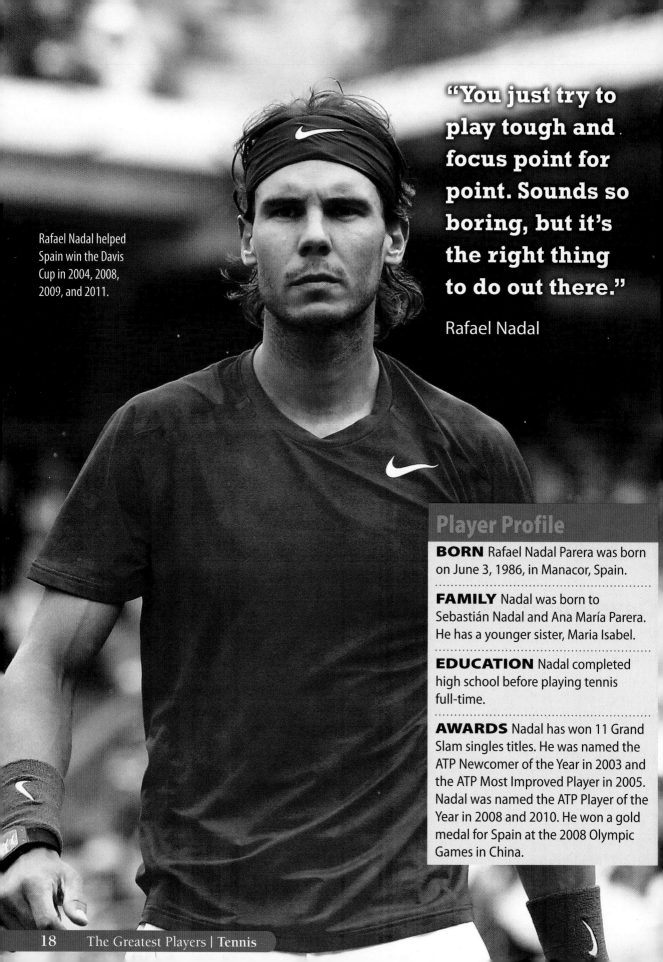

Rafael Nadal helped Spain win the Davis Cup in 2004, 2008, 2009, and 2011.

"You just try to play tough and focus point for point. Sounds so boring, but it's the right thing to do out there."

Rafael Nadal

Player Profile

BORN Rafael Nadal Parera was born on June 3, 1986, in Manacor, Spain.

FAMILY Nadal was born to Sebastián Nadal and Ana María Parera. He has a younger sister, Maria Isabel.

EDUCATION Nadal completed high school before playing tennis full-time.

AWARDS Nadal has won 11 Grand Slam singles titles. He was named the ATP Newcomer of the Year in 2003 and the ATP Most Improved Player in 2005. Nadal was named the ATP Player of the Year in 2008 and 2010. He won a gold medal for Spain at the 2008 Olympic Games in China.

Rafael Nadal
Spain

Early Years

Rafael Nadal's uncle Toni Nadal was a former tennis player. He began teaching Nadal how to play tennis at age 3. Nadal was 8 years old when he won a regional tennis championship for children under 12. At age 12, Nadal won tennis titles in Spain and Europe for his age group.

Nadal joined the **International Tennis Federation** junior circuit in 2001. He was 15 years old. The next year, he reached the semi-final round of the Wimbledon junior boys' singles tournament. In 2002, Nadal won his first match during an ATP event. He became the ninth player in the Open Era to win an ATP match before the age of 16. Nadal played in the Wimbledon men's singles tournament the next year, at age 17. He became the youngest player to reach the semi-final round in 19 years.

Developing Skills

Nadal won his first ATP Tour event in August 2004. The tournament was held on a clay court in Poland. Nadal won all 10 sets he played at the tournament. He won his first Grand Slam singles title at the French Open in 2005. Nadal defeated the world's number one ranked player Roger Federer in the semi-final at the tournament. That season, Nadal won 11 ATP singles titles. He was 19. It set a record for most ATP tournament wins in a season by a teenager.

Nadal was the number two ranked tennis player in the world at the end of the 2005 season. He was ranked number two at the end of every season for the next six years. Nadal has won 600 matches and lost 123 during his ATP career. He has won 53 ATP titles, including 11 Grand Slam titles. He has won at least one Grand Slam tournament every year since 2005.

Rafael Nadal

Greatest Moment

Nadal and Roger Federer met in the final at Wimbledon for the third straight year in 2008. Federer won the previous two years. Nadal defeated Federer in five sets. The match took four hours and 48 minutes to play. It is the longest final match in Wimbledon men's singles history.

Nadal defeated Novak Djokovic in the final of the French Open in 2012. It was his seventh French Open singles title. The victory set a record for most men's singles titles at the tournament.

In 2007, Rafael Nadal extended his record of consecutive match wins on clay courts to 81. This streak helped Nadal earn the nickname, "The King of Clay."

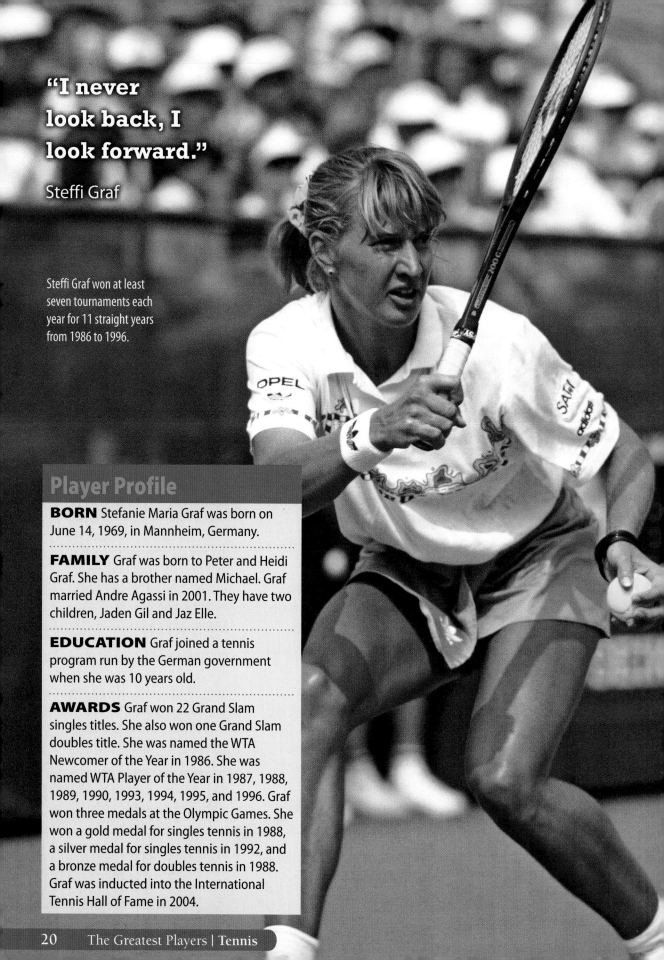

> **"I never look back, I look forward."**
>
> Steffi Graf

Steffi Graf won at least seven tournaments each year for 11 straight years from 1986 to 1996.

Player Profile

BORN Stefanie Maria Graf was born on June 14, 1969, in Mannheim, Germany.

FAMILY Graf was born to Peter and Heidi Graf. She has a brother named Michael. Graf married Andre Agassi in 2001. They have two children, Jaden Gil and Jaz Elle.

EDUCATION Graf joined a tennis program run by the German government when she was 10 years old.

AWARDS Graf won 22 Grand Slam singles titles. She also won one Grand Slam doubles title. She was named the WTA Newcomer of the Year in 1986. She was named WTA Player of the Year in 1987, 1988, 1989, 1990, 1993, 1994, 1995, and 1996. Graf won three medals at the Olympic Games. She won a gold medal for singles tennis in 1988, a silver medal for singles tennis in 1992, and a bronze medal for doubles tennis in 1988. Graf was inducted into the International Tennis Hall of Fame in 2004.

Steffi Graf
Germany

Early Years

Steffi Graf's father gave her a wooden tennis racket when she was 3 years old. He began coaching her to play tennis. Graf entered her first tennis tournament at age 5. By age 12, she became the first German player to win the Junior Orange Bowl International Tennis Championship.

Graf became a professional tennis player in October 1982. She was 13 years old. Graf won her first professional tournament that year at the Porsche Grand Prix in Germany. She finished the year as the 124th ranked tennis player. Graf became the second youngest player in history to earn an international ranking. She won her first WTA singles title in 1986. Graf won nine tournaments that year. She finished the season ranked number three in the world, behind Chris Evert and Martina Navratilova.

Developing Skills

Graf won her first Grand Slam singles title in 1987. She defeated Martina Navratilova in the final of the French Open. Graf won 11 tournaments that year. She became the top ranked women's tennis player for the first time in August 1987. She held the top ranking for a record 186 straight weeks. During her career, Graf was ranked number one in the world for a record total of 377 weeks.

Graf won more than 900 matches during her career. She won 107 singles titles on the WTA Tour. She played in the final round of 31 Grand Slam singles tournaments. Graf retired in August 1999.

Steffi Graf

Greatest Moment

Graf won the gold medal for women's singles tennis at the Olympic Games in 1988. She also won the Australian Open, the French Open, Wimbledon, and the U.S. Open that year. Graf is the only tennis player in history to win all Grand Slam events and an Olympic gold medal in the same year. The feat is now called the Golden Grand Slam.

Steffi Graf finished the year as the number one ranked women's tennis player in the world eight times.

"I let my racket do the talking. That's what I am about, really. I just go out and win tennis matches."

Pete Sampras

Pete Sampras won a Grand Slam title as a teenager, in his 20s, and in his 30s. Only one other tennis player has accomplished the same feat.

Player Profile

BORN Petros Sampras was born on August 12, 1971, in Washington, D.C.

FAMILY Sampras was born to Sam and Georgia Sampras. He has an older sister named Stella and an older brother named Gus. He has a younger sister named Marion. Sampras married Bridgette Wilson in September 2000. They have two sons, Christian and Ryan.

EDUCATION Sampras left high school to play tennis full-time.

AWARDS Sampras won 14 Grand Slam singles titles. He was inducted into the International Tennis Hall of Fame in 2007.

Pete Sampras
United States

Early Years

Pete Sampras's family moved from Washington, D.C. to California when he was young. He started playing tennis in Rancho Palos Verdes, California when he was 7 years old. His father took him to a local tennis club to find a coach. Pete Fischer began training Sampras. Sampras lost his first junior match for players under the age of 12: 6-0, 6-0. Sampras continued to practice and soon became one of the top ranked junior players in the United States.

Sampras was chosen to play on the U.S. Junior Davis Cup team in 1987. He became a professional tennis player the next year. He was 16 years old. Sampras played in 13 ATP events during his first year as a professional. He lost in the first round of six tournaments. He finished the year winning 10 matches and losing 10 matches.

Developing Skills

Sampras became known for his powerful serve. In 1990, he won his first ATP singles title at an indoor tournament in Philadelphia. Sampras also won his first Grand Slam singles title at the U.S. Open that year. He defeated Andre Agassi in three sets to win the championship. Sampras was 19 years old. He became the youngest player ever to win the U.S. Open. He finished the year ranked number five in the world.

Sampras was the number one ranked player in the world for six consecutive years from 1993 to 1998. Sampras played on the ATP Tour for 14 years. He won 64 singles titles during his career. He broke the record for most career Grand Slam men's singles titles when he won Wimbledon in 2000.

Pete Sampras

Greatest Moment

Sampras defeated Patrick Rafter of Australia in four sets to win the Wimbledon singles title in 2000. It was his seventh Wimbledon championship. The victory tied a record for most men's singles titles in a career at Wimbledon.

Sampras faced Andre Agassi in the final of the U.S. Open in 2002. Sampras hit 144 **aces** during the tournament. He hit 33 aces in the final to win in four sets. He was 31 years old, making him the oldest player to win a Grand Slam singles title in 32 years. It was Sampras's last ATP title. It also tied a record for most wins at the U.S. Open.

Pete Sampras was named the U.S. Olympic Committee "Sportsman of the Year" in 1997. He was the first tennis player to ever receive the award.

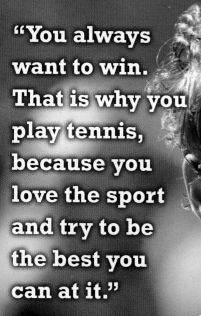

> "You always want to win. That is why you play tennis, because you love the sport and try to be the best you can at it."
>
> Roger Federer

Roger Federer has won the ATPWorldTour.com Fans' Favorite Award a record 10 consecutive times from 2003 to 2012.

Player Profile

BORN Roger Federer was born on August 8, 1981, in Basel, Switzerland.

FAMILY Federer was born to Robert and Lynette Federer. He has an older sister named Diana. Federer married female tennis player Mirka Vavrinec in 2009. They have twin girls, Charlene Riva and Myla Rose.

EDUCATION Federer left his home and joined the Swiss Tennis development program when he was 13 years old.

AWARDS Federer has won 17 Grand Slam singles titles. He won the ATP Stefan Edberg Sportsmanship Award in 2004, 2005, 2006, 2007, 2008, 2009, 2011, and 2012. Federer was named the International Tennis Federation Player of the Year in 2004, 2005, 2006, 2007, and 2009.

Roger Federer
Switzerland

Early Years

Roger Federer started playing tennis with his parents and sister. He joined a junior tennis program at age 8. By the time Federer was 11 years old, he was one of the top three junior players in Switzerland. In 1994, Federer left his home to train at the Swiss National Tennis Center.

Federer joined the International Tennis Federation junior tennis circuit in 1996. He won the Wimbledon boys' singles title and doubles title in 1998. He also won the Junior Orange Bowl International Tennis Championship that year. He became the number one ranked junior player in the world. At the end of the year, he became a professional tennis player.

Developing Skills

Federer won his first ATP singles title in 2001. It was the only tournament he won that year. He won his first Grand Slam singles title at Wimbledon in 2003. Federer won his second Grand Slam singles title at the Australian Open in 2004. The victory made him the number one ranked player in the world. He won 10 more ATP tournaments that year, including Wimbledon and the U.S. Open.

Federer remained the number one ranked player in the world for 237 weeks. It set a record for most consecutive weeks in the top spot of the ATP Tour rankings. Federer also has the ATP record for most total weeks ranked number one in a career with 302. Federer has won 76 singles titles on the ATP Tour. His 17 Grand Slam singles titles are more than any other male tennis player.

Roger Federer

Greatest Moment

Federer played in the final round of the French Open in 2006, 2007, and 2008. He lost each time to Rafael Nadal. He made it to the final round again in 2009 and won the French Open singles title for the first time. The victory made Federer a champion at all four Grand Slam events. He is one of seven male tennis players to win the singles title at all four Grand Slam events during a career.

In 2012, Federer defeated Andy Murray in the final round of Wimbledon in four sets. It was Federer's seventh singles title at Wimbledon. The win tied the record for most Wimbledon men's championships.

Roger Federer set a record by winning 10 or more ATP singles titles in three consecutive years. He accomplished the feat between 2004 and 2006.

Greatest Moments

1973
Billie Jean King creates the Women's Tennis Association to help women tennis players earn the same amount of money as men.

1881
The U.S. National Championship is held for the first time. The tournament eventually becomes the U.S. Open.

1891
The French Championships is held for the first time. The event is now held at the Stade de Roland Garros in Paris and is known as the French Open.

1968
The Open Era begins. Rod Laver is the first professional tennis player to win the Wimbledon men's title.

1875   **1900**   **1925**   **1950**   **1960**   **1970**

1877
The Wimbledon Championships is played for the first time. It is held at the All England Croquet and Lawn Tennis Club.

1905
The Lawn Tennis Association of Australasia holds its first tournament for men. An event for women is added in 1922. The tournament is now called the Australian Open.

1972
The Association of Tennis Professionals creates a series of tournaments for male players. The ATP ranking system is created in August 1973.

1973
Billie Jean King defeats Bobby Riggs in the "Battle of the Sexes" tennis match in front of 30,000 people.

1980 – Borg vs. McEnroe

When: July 5, 1980

Where: London, England

The Wimbledon men's singles final in 1980 takes three hours and 53 minutes to play. Björn Borg and John McEnroe play a 34-point tie breaker in the fourth set. McEnroe wins the tie-breaker 18-16 to force a final and deciding fifth set. Borg wins the last set 8-6. It is his 35th straight match win at the Grand Slam event and his fifth straight men's singles title at Wimbledon.

1984 – Lendl's Comeback

When: June 10, 1984

Where: Paris, France

John McEnroe has a match record of 82-3 during the 1984 season. He wins 13 titles this year, including Wimbledon and the U.S. Open. In the final of the French Open, he wins the first two sets against Ivan Lendl. Lendl comes back to win the next three sets and defeats McEnroe.

1980 — 1990 — 2000 — 2010 — 2015

1988
Steffi Graf defeats Gabriela Sabatini of Argentina in the U.S. Open. The two players meet again for in the women's singles final at the Olympic Games in Seoul, South Korea. Graf wins the gold medal in straight sets.

2012 – Djokovic vs. Nadal

When: January 29, 2012

Where: Melbourne, Australia

Novak Djokovic enters the Australian Open as the defending champion and the number one ranked player in the world. It is the first time a player other than Roger Federer or Rafael Nadal is ranked number one since 2003. Djokovic loses the first set in the final round 7-5 to Nadal. Djokovic wins the next two sets, but loses the fourth set. Djokovic wins the final set 7-5. The match takes five hours and 53 minutes to play. Djokovic wins the Australian Open again in 2013. He becomes the first player in the Open Era to win three consecutive Australian Open men's singles titles.

Write a Biography

Life Story

A person's life story can be the subject of a book. This kind of book is called a biography. Biographies often describe the lives of people who have achieved great success. These people may be alive today, or they may have lived many years ago. Reading a biography can help you learn more about a great person.

Get the Facts

Use this book, and research in the library and on the Internet, to find out more about your favorite tennis player. Learn as much about this player as you can. What tournaments did this person play in? What are his or her statistics in important categories? Has this person set any records? Also, be sure to write down key events in the person's life. What was this person's childhood like? What has he or she accomplished? Is there anything else that makes this person special or unusual?

Andy Murray won a gold medal for Great Britain at the 2012 Olympic Games in London. He defeated Roger Federer in the men's singles tennis final.

Use the Concept Web

A concept web is a useful research tool. Read the questions in the concept web on the following page. Answer the questions in your notebook. Your answers will help you write a biography.

Concept Web

- What did you learn from the books you read in your research?
- Would you suggest these books to others?
- Was anything missing from these books?

- Where does this individual currently reside?
- Does he or she have a family?

- Where and when was this person born?
- Describe his or her parents, siblings, and friends.
- Did this person grow up in unusual circumstances?

Your Opinion

Adulthood

Childhood

WRITING A BIOGRAPHY

Main Accomplishments

Help and Obstacles

Work and Preparation

- What is this person's life's work?
- Has he or she received awards or recognition for accomplishments?
- How have this person's accomplishments served others?

- Did this individual have a positive attitude?
- Did he or she receive help from others?
- Did this person have a mentor?
- Did this person face any hardships?
- If so, how were the hardships overcome?

- What was this person's education?
- What was his or her work experience?
- How does this person work; what is the process he or she uses?

Know your STUFF!

1 How many straight Wimbledon titles did Björn Borg win?

2 Who holds the record for most singles and doubles titles in a career?

3 How many people watched Billie Jean King and Bobby Riggs play in "The Battle of the Sexes" on television?

4 Which male tennis player has won the most Grand Slam singles titles?

5 How many tennis balls did Andre Agassi hit each day when he was young?

6 How many tournaments did Chris Evert win in her first year as a professional tennis player?

7 Why did Billie Jean King start the WTA in 1973?

8 How old was Rafael Nadal when he won his first match at an ATP event?

9 How many aces did Pete Sampras hit during the U.S. Open in 2002?

10 What is the Open Era?

ANSWERS: 1. Five **2.** Martina Navratilova **3.** 50 million **4.** Roger Federer **5.** 3,000 **6.** 12 **7.** King started the WTA to help women tennis players earn the same prize money as men **8.** 15 **9.** 144 **10.** The Open Era began in 1968 when professional tennis players were allowed to compete in Grand Slam tournaments

Key Words

aces: a point scored from the serve when the opposing player does not hit the ball

amateur: a player who does not compete for money

Association of Tennis Professionals (ATP): a group created to organize tournaments and develop a ranking system for male professional tennis players

Australian Open: a major tennis championship held every year in Melbourne, Australia, for male and female players

backhand: a shot where the back of the hand is facing the direction the ball will travel

Davis Cup: a competition held every year between tennis teams from different countries around the world

doubles: tennis matches where two people play against two other people

Fed Cup Award of Excellence: an award presented to past or present members of a women's national tennis team that competed in the annual Fed Cup and represents the spirit of competition

forehand: a shot where the palm of the hand is facing the direction the ball will travel

French Open: a major tennis championship held every year in Paris, France, for male and female players

Grand Slam: winning all four major tennis championships

International Tennis Federation: an organization created to oversee events and rules for both amateur and professional tennis players around the world

professional: an athlete who gets paid to play a sport

serve: a shot from behind the baseline that begins play in a tennis game

singles: tennis matches where one person plays against another person

slump: a stretch of bad play by a player or team that usually results in losing

table tennis: a game similar to tennis that is played on a table with small wood paddles and a small plastic ball

U.S. Open: a major tennis championship held every year in Flushing, New York, for both male and female players

Wimbledon Championships: a major tennis championship held every year in London, England, for both male and female players

Women's Tennis Association (WTA): a group created to organize tournaments for female professional tennis players and help them earn the same amount of money as male tennis players

Index

Log on to www.av2books.com

AV[2] by Weigl brings you media enhanced books that support active learning. Go to www.av2books.com, and enter the special code found on page 2 of this book. You will gain access to enriched and enhanced content that supplements and complements this book. Content includes video, audio, weblinks, quizzes, a slide show, and activities.

AV[2] Online Navigation

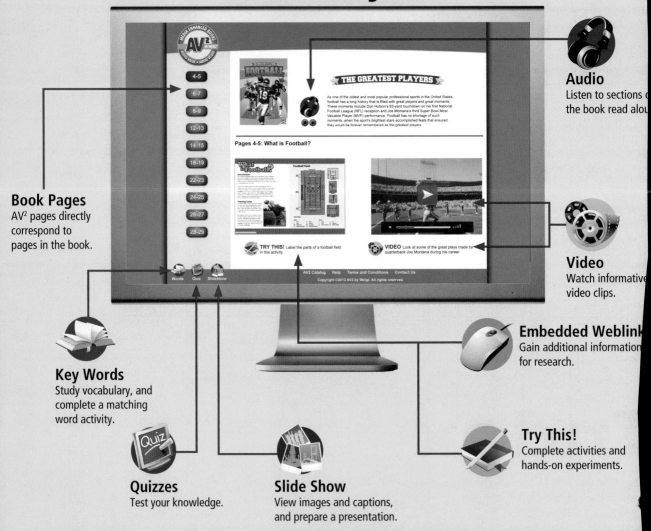

Book Pages
AV[2] pages directly correspond to pages in the book.

Audio
Listen to sections of the book read alou

Video
Watch informative video clips.

Key Words
Study vocabulary, and complete a matching word activity.

Embedded Weblink
Gain additional information for research.

Quizzes
Test your knowledge.

Slide Show
View images and captions, and prepare a presentation.

Try This!
Complete activities and hands-on experiments.

AV[2] was built to bridge the gap between print and digital. We encourage you to tell us what you like and what you want to see in the future.

Sign up to be an AV[2] Ambassador at www.av2books.com/ambassador.